Guidebooks for Counsellors

Counsellors in the course of their practice are likely to come across clients with particular difficulties, such as experience of incest, drug or alcohol addiction, or eating difficulties. These issues may not be the main focus of the counselling and it may not be appropriate to refer the client on to a specialist in one of these fields, if such exists locally. There may be literature available but little guidance for the counsellor seeking it.

The Publications Sub-Committee of the British Association for Counselling are publishing a series of booklets to help counsellors in this situation. Written by specialist counsellors or therapists, they draw attention to issues which are likely to arise for the client and for the counsellor and which may be missed by the novice. They also provide a guide to the relevant literature. Being brief, readable and to the point it is hoped that counsellors will be able to consult them even when time and money are short. In this way it is hoped that these booklets will contribute to the raising of standards of counselling in general.

The Sub-Committee would like to thank not only those members who worked to produce these booklets, but also Isobel Palmer and Sally Cook, and the consultant editors, myself, Judith Baron, Stephen Palmer and Moira Walker, whose contribution was vital.

Julia Segal, Chair
Publications Sub-Committee of the
British Association for Counselling

GW00771346

Peter Dale

Peter Dale originally trained in psychiatric social work, and subsequently in Gestalt psychotherapy and counselling. He has been involved in individual and group therapy for adults who were abused as children since 1985, as well as supervising the work of other counsellors and therapists. A particularly valuable theoretical and therapeutic influence was a training course at the Giarretto Institute, the sexual abuse treatment programme in San José, California in 1987. This provided a vision and experience of the enormous recovery and creative potential of abused people.

Peter is an established author and trainer and has over 20 publications relating to assessment and treatment of child abuse. He is a British Association for Counselling Accredited Counsellor and has a private therapeutic and supervisory practice in Hastings, East Sussex. He is currently engaged in a doctoral research project at the University of Brighton on the effectiveness of therapy with adults who were abused as children.

Counselling Adults who were Abused as Children

Peter Dale

British Association for Counselling
1 Regent Place • Rugby • Warwickshire CV21 2PJ
Office 0788 550899 • Information Line 0788 578328 • Fax 0788 562189

© **BAC 1993**   **ISBN 0 946181 40 3**

Published by the British Association for Counselling, 1 Regent Place, Rugby,
Warwickshire CV21 2PJ

First printed 1993

Produced by   BAC, a Registered Charity number 298361
Printed by   Quorn Litho, Queens Road, Loughborough,
                   Leicestershire LE11 1HH

Others in the series:

Counselling People in Eating Distress

British Association for Counselling

- Codes of Ethics & Practice for Counsellors, for Counselling Skills,
  for Trainers, for the Supervision of Counsellors
- Counselling publications mail order service
- Quarterly journal with in-depth articles, news and views of
  members
- Individual Accreditation, Supervisor Recognition and Counsellor
  Course Recognition schemes

Join BAC now - the Voice of Counselling

Details of the above and much more besides:
BAC, 1 Regent Place, Rugby CV21 2PJ
Tel: 0788 550899

Contents

Foreword

There is an increasing awareness that many people who present themselves to helping professionals are suffering from the effects and consequences of childhood abuse.

Peter Dale has written this booklet with a clarity which will give confidence to counsellors and therapists who may lack experience in this specific area and may feel daunted by the task ahead.

I have had the privilege of working with Peter and know that this booklet is written from a broad base of theoretical knowledge, as well as extensive professional experience of working in this field. This combination brings an understanding of the wide range of consequences faced by both men and women who have been abused. He takes the reader through the therapeutic journey with skill and sensitivity, and shares the insights he has gained from extensive clinical practice. By personal example he clearly demonstrates how a sensitive and empathic counsellor, together with a committed client, can overcome the effects of abuse. He describes in a hopeful and positive way how a client can progress to becoming not only a survivor but one who discovers hidden strengths and creativity in their life.

As a doctor I am aware that general practitioners and hospital specialists often meet patients with confusing physical symptoms which have their origins in childhood trauma. General practitioners are increasingly employing counsellors and I feel that this booklet will be invaluable to them as well as to all therapists who are working with the legacy of abuse.

Mary Rees, MB, BS, DObsRCOG,
member Institute of Psychosexual Medicine
Senior Clinical Medical Officer,
Hastings & Rother NHS Trust

Preface

Whilst a good many publications have appeared in recent years relating to adults who were abused as children, much of this material has been weighted towards theoretical discussion regarding the causation of child abuse and descriptions of common consequences of abuse.

In running training courses for several years in this field, it has never been possible to recommend a single source which focuses on the 'nuts and bolts' of common experiences and dilemmas in working with adults who were abused as children, for counsellors who have little direct experience in this area. I hope that this booklet will go a short way towards meeting this need.

In writing it, I have been conscious of a desire to avoid using the terms 'victims' or 'survivors'. Somehow these terms, especially 'victim', are limiting and do not sufficiently reflect the creative recovery potential of the people I have worked with. Instead I have stayed with the rather more laborious 'adults abused as children'. In the interests of brevity I have also sidestepped theoretical dilemmas about postulated differences between counselling and psychotherapy and use the terms interchangeably.

I have attempted to write the booklet in gender neutral language. A lot of the time 'she's and 'he's are interchangeable, except where the context makes this obviously not so. I am concerned that skills and services develop to meet the needs of abused people of both genders. However, I would not want this to imply that males are not the predominant sexual abusers of children.

I would like to briefly acknowledge the great personal and professional support of my partner and colleague Veronica Locke; and the resilience of my children Nathan, Rory and Rosanna.

Whilst the views expressed in this book are those of the author, I would like to acknowledge the support and facilities of the NSPCC, in particular my colleagues for a number of years in the NSPCC East Sussex Team, Ron, Kay, Yvonne and David.

And then the day came

When the risk to remain tight

In a bud was more painful

Than the risk it took to blossom...

(anon) [1]

Introduction

Counsellors in all settings increasingly hear directly from their clients that they were abused in some way when they were children. Such abuse may have been physical, sexual, emotional, neglect, or any combination of these. Other clients may report a vague sense of unease about childhood memories which they cannot quite bring into focus - although this haze may be sporadically punctuated by violent and lurid images and nightmares. Alternatively, some clients may have no conscious memory of abuse and may refute any suggestion of this being a possibility, yet their specific problems may leave the counsellor wondering whether significant abuse-related material is being repressed.

It is not uncommon for otherwise experienced counsellors to feel somewhat inadequate at the prospect of working with a client who was abused as a child, or when significant abuse issues arise with existing clients. It is the primary aim of this booklet to provide a theoretical and practical context so that such anxiety need not impede the effective development of the helping relationship. Whilst specialist knowledge and skills are important, no counsellor or therapist has ever acquired these without first of all having to work from a position of inexperience.

Many adults who were abused as children are very selective as to whom they first disclose their abuse and choose a person they intuitively feel willing to risk trusting. If an existing client reveals a history of abuse, this can be an indicator that the counselling has reached a very important stage - not that the client necessarily needs to be referred to someone else with more experience. Anxious reactions to refer elsewhere because one feels inadequate or because one wants the client to have the 'best possible service' may be perceived by clients as a rejection and may be counter-productive to the repair of the initial damage to trust in their lives.

Such concerns on the part of the counsellor may be better responded to by specialist supervision or consultation whilst direct work with the client continues. At such times, and throughout all of the therapeutic process, it is important not to minimise the importance of the core conditions of counselling and therapy: the congruence and genuineness of the counsellor, unconditional positive regard for the client and the development and communication of empathic understanding.

At the point of seeking help, the basic but profound experience of being *listened to* may have enormous impact. Rogers and subsequent writers in the person-centred counselling tradition suggest that the existence of the core conditions may be 'enough' for clients in counselling relationships to make desired changes. I suspect that on occasions this can be so, and the experience for many distressed people of being *really listened to* in the spirit of the core conditions with their anti-technical and purely human qualities can be profoundly moving and positively helpful. However, for people who were abused as children - especially those who were severely, multiply and chronically abused - the impact of the core conditions alone is unlikely to be sufficient to help resolve their wide range of emotional, relationship and cognitive problems.

Counselling adults who were abused as children inevitably involves a focus on vulnerability and the often devastating consequences of abuse. However, it is equally about focussing on resilience and strength. This requires tremendous courage and, thankfully, a high proportion of abused people who seek therapy find the determination and the commitment to see it through. Consequently, there are genuine grounds for counsellors to maintain optimistic attitudes towards the prospect of recovery. The generation of an atmosphere of hope and support is a key component of the therapeutic relationship.

In the description of consequences of abuse which follows, it is important to be aware that many of these are normal human responses to traumatic events and stresses. Adults who were abused as children, tend to endure such consequences more intensely and chronically. If some of the material in this book is painful for you, please take it slowly, look after yourself, and discuss it in your own supervision or therapy.

Counselling Adults who were Abused as Children

Consequences of Abuse

Many of the consequences of abuse involve the continuation in adult life and relationships, of feelings and patterns of behaviour which were utilised at the time of the abuse, as vital survival strategies. These coping mechanisms are learned at a time of high emotional arousal and become imprinted deeply into the developing personality. It is important not to under-estimate the historical *value* of such defences, even when in adult life they are *disadvantageous* in the search for productive, satisfying lives and relationships. Processes vital for physical and emotional survival as an abused child, can amount to significant handicaps for adults attempting to develop and sustain intimate relationships.

Not surprisingly, the prospect of change which requires a review of the need for, and value of, such defences, often creates powerful conscious and unconscious resistances. Preference for the painful familiar, as opposed to the anxieties associated with change, is an experience most people have shared at some time in their lives. Positive change does not flow from the counsellor doing a 'demolition job' on these defences. Change occurs from work which enables the client to become aware of their extent and significance, and gradually to experiment with alternative patterns of construing, experiencing and communicating. The therapeutic relationship provides the 'safe container' for a gentle and gradual dismantling of obsolete parts of the fortress.

Physical consequences

A wide range of somatic and psycho-somatic symptoms are known to be associated with abuse and the defences of the body to survive it [2]. Commonly reported physical associations with childhood abuse include many of the following: sleep disturbances, chronic muscle tensions, jaw/joint tensions, regular headaches, genital-urinary problems, frequent infections, menstrual irregularities, vaginismus, skin complaints, seizures, palpitations, dizziness, gastro-intestinal problems, eating disorders, anxiety attacks, depression, mood swings, a wide variety of compulsive and obsessional behaviours, substance abuse, and self-injury.

Physical symptoms may be the residue of learned and habitual responses of chronic anxiety, hyper-vigilance, over- or under-breathing, which perpetuate in adult life and may respond quickly to the teaching of relaxation, visualisation, or self-hypnotic techniques. However clients who experience significant physical complaints should be under continuing medical supervision during counselling. Clarkson has warned of the dangers of assumptions being made regarding psychosomatic processes:

"It is imperative to take a full and complete medical history to avoid the kind of situation (which actually happened) where a counsellor kept working on a client's 'angry headaches', neglecting to involve medical practitioners. The client eventually died of a brain tumour whilst still in the care of the counsellor concerned..." [3]

Powerful cognitive distortions may result in many sexual abuse victims *blaming their bodies* for the abuse - for being attractive, for developing sexual characteristics, for responding sexually. Self-punitive behaviour may follow: anorexia, bulimia, substance abuse, risk-taking behaviour, and self-mutilation. Self-mutilation, especially cutting to draw blood, may have a tension-relieving function, or may serve to distract from other feelings. People who self-mutilate sometimes comment that the physical pain is preferable to, or easier to handle, than the internal emotional pain. Self-mutilation may also be the client's way of re-orientating or 'grounding' during an involuntary dissociative experience (see page 13). Addictive and compulsive behaviours can serve to deaden or distract the mind from overwhelming painful emotions or intolerable critical internal self-talk.

Emotional Consequences

Emotional deprivation, damage and impaired emotional development stem from the combined impact of the repeated trauma and the abusing environment of the home and family relationships. Difficulties are common regarding the *recognition*, the *understanding*, and the *expression* of feelings. Clients may describe a state of emotional numbness - having no feelings at all, or they may report chronically deadened sensations as if the feeling volume - control is turned down. Such deadening or flattening of affect may include every aspect of emotional life - resulting in an inability to experience pleasure as well as hurt. Associated with such experiences there may be unpredictable mood swings, including explosive outbursts of rage, tearfulness and despair. Sudden suicidal impulses may occur. A frequently used metaphor is that of the *unexploded bomb* - describing the intensity of repressed emotion and the fear of being overwhelmed by painful and angry feelings.

Emotional development can be significantly affected by childhood abusive experiences. There may be an absence, loss or curtailment of naturally paced developmental stages. The spontaneous unfolding of the individual child's natural pace of development becomes disjointed through repeated trauma and the lack of a secure environment. Key aspects of emotional development may be retarded or frozen and others may be precociously advanced resulting in a state of inappropriate *pseudo-maturity*.

Pseudo-maturity involves segments of emotional development being artificially accelerated. Many children acquire an overwhelming sense of responsibility for others at a very early age. The child may have a parenting role with siblings and sometimes with his or her own parents as well - becoming a 'parental child'. Such children often become very perceptive about the feelings and needs of others and believe that it is their duty to meet such needs. In acquiring and adapting to this role they sacrifice their ability to recognise and respond to their own needs. Such highly developed intuition about the moods, feelings and thoughts of significant others around them enables children to 'read the tea leaves' in order to adapt themselves in ways which minimise the likelihood of an abusive incident occurring. In counselling, clients may express guilt feelings and shame about incidents where physical abuse was looming and where to avoid this, they had behaved in ways which led to sexual abuse instead - this being preferable to the child at the time than another beating.

Pseudo-maturity is also often conspicuous in the area of sexual development. There are two major types of incest dynamics: the 'tyrannical type' and the 'pseudo-affectionate' type. In the tyrannical type, the sexual abuse is invariably associated with physical illtreatment. Both are brutal and likely to involve all family members. The child is physically coerced into sexual acts by physical violence and threats of it. Children do not tell because of threats to their own safety and that of others. Children experience and learn an early association between sex and pain/violence, and may suffer in adult life from aversions to sex/men, or sometimes from only being able to achieve sexual arousal in the context of pain and violence. For some, the seeds of adult extremes of masochism and sadism may be sown by such childhood abuse.

In the 'pseudo-affectionate' type of abuse, the child is deliberately prematurely sexualised by the abuser. It is clear from research and therapy with sexual offenders that they use deliberate and sophisticated manoeuvres to induce children into sex, to maintain children in such relationships, and to prevent them from seeking and obtaining effective protection. The abuser may be the parent with the prime caretaking role for the young child. Within the context of legitimate physical caretaking, such abusers gradually introduce subtle sexual stimulation of the child's erogenous zones under the guise of 'tickling' and 'games'. Bodies being designed as bodies are (and many adults who were abused as children will blame themselves terribly in later life for this) the young child finds this to be a playful, arousing and enjoyable experience.

Subtly and gradually, the 'games' become more explicitly sexual and the child is introduced to the experience of sexual excitement and pleasure in a variety of forms. Compliance is induced by messages such as 'This is our special secret...' or 'Don't tell anyone or Daddy will be sent to jail...' We shall return to the long-term effects of such messages later. However the fact that the young child has been deliberately trained to enjoy and seek sexual sensations and pleasure with another creates the sexual pseudo-maturity. The pseudo-affectionate experience of sexual abuse leaves victims with disabling feelings of shame, guilt and self-blame, and this is especially so in the sorts of abuse where, as we have seen, some sexual pleasure is experience. Victims have no awareness of the subtle processes of entrapment, all they remember is their own responses which may have included learned seductiveness, initiation of sexual activity and receiving material rewards for sex.

Whilst the sexual abuse victim who was abused in a tyrannical context may hold more consistently negative and hateful feelings towards the abuser and other family members, the 'pseudo-affectionate' abuse victim often struggles with intense feelings of ambivalence. The abuser may well have been the primary caretaker, and the victim may remember many positive experiences and qualities within that relationship which may continue in the present day. If the abuse came to light during childhood and the child and the abuser were separated, the victim may have experienced a significant sense of loss. The way in which 'protection' occurred, or did not occur, is also likely to have had a major impact. Unfortunately, many abused children who came to the notice of child protection agencies did not, and often still do not, receive appropriate services relative to their needs and wishes. Far too frequently, the actions of the 'protection' agencies and systems are themselves perceived by child abuse victims as being unhelpful and damaging [4]. This may include multiple foster homes or placement in institutions, both of which may result in further abuse for the child. Such *institutional abuse* of children is currently the focus of growing public concern.

The emotional consequences of abuse can profoundly damage one's early sense of security. There is an absence of a stage of trusting dependency and safe initial exploration of the world from the basis of a permanent 'nest'. The sense for the child is of the nest falling apart. This results in the development of an inner agony related to the physical trauma of the abuse and chronic anxiety through the lack of security and unmet dependency needs which can only be handled by adaptive responses of sedation and distraction. The profound processes of dissociation and splitting begin to be established (see page 11). From this perspective the damage done at this time to aspects of emotional development such as the ability to trust, results in a petrification of that developmental stage in a timeless vacuum: the dilemma regarding willingness to trust of the 41 year old abused person who begins therapy may be as it was at the age the person was traumatised.

Cognitive Consequences

Being chronically abused within an abusing family amounts to a process of systematic brainwashing in addition to the impact of the traumatic events themselves. A coercive distorted belief system is imposed and the child is deprived of the developmental opportunity of exploring and learning to trust its own perceptions in relation to a relatively consistent external reality.

Cognitive injunctions
In most chronic abuse scenarios, powerful parental messages - or *injunctions* - are a component of the abusing actions. The damage caused by such injunctions is that they are introjected by the child at a time of high emotional arousal stemming from hyper-vigilance, anxiety and fear. Because of the degree of arousal, repetition and parental source of such messages, they are deeply learned and become incorporated into the child's own sense of self. Key self-defeating injunctions with this origin may re-play in the client's mind in adult life as if they were pre-recorded audio tapes to which there is no access to the 'on' and 'off' buttons. Working to identify, revise and eradicate

such 'tapes' will be an important part of the cognitive aspect of the therapy.

Calof[5] has outlined a series of key injunctions through which abused children are taught to acquire a set of inappropriate beliefs about themselves. These include:

- Total unquestioning obedience to parental, and often also religious and educational, authority;
- Statements such as: *'All children do this...' 'You are enjoying it...' 'It's your fault - for being cute/pretty/sexy...' 'You are bad/worthless/ unlovable...' 'Be loyal to the family at all costs...' 'Don't show pain...' 'Stay in control...' 'Don't think about or reflect upon your situation...' 'Don't ask for help...' 'Don't have needs - put others' before your own...' 'Love means being hurt...'*, etc.

The introjection of a combination of such messages and injunctions constitutes a significant social and emotional handicap: **life as a whole becomes experienced and interpreted through this distorting filter.** This establishes and enhances a marked tendency to *misperceive* the behaviour, attitudes and motives of others in all interpersonal encounters.

Cognitive defences
As part of the inherent survival instinct, cognitive defences are constructed. These prevent the personality from being overwhelmed and disintegrating and as such are adaptive and vital at the time of the abuse. The most common cognitive defences are denial (including minimisation and rationalisation), splitting and dissociation.

Denial involves an acquired belief that the abuse did not happen, or that if it did happen, that it was not abusive or damaging. In most forms of chronic abuse there are powerful internal family forces which restrain the child from telling outsiders. This may involve significant fearful threats to the child such as: *'If you tell, no one will believe you... I will kill you, your mother, your pet...' etc.* Or, appealing to an induced inappropriate sense of family responsibility: *'If you tell, I will kill myself... go to prison... we will lose the house... your sisters and brothers will be taken away...'* etc.

False retractions, in addition to the above pressures, are often promoted by the inadequate nature of child protection systems. Having perhaps plucked up courage to tell a teacher about ongoing sexual abuse, the child may find that it is he or she who is whisked away from home into a strange environment and subjected to all forms of unexplained intrusive investigatory ordeals. The significance of such events is that the individual psychological denial of the child is further reinforced. The mistrust of outsiders - including 'helping' professionals - is compounded by this. If, in later life, help is sought for abuse-related problems, this mistrust is likely to be a significant factor in the therapeutic process.

Denial often also occurs for victims who, whilst aware of the abuse, believe that this has not had any detrimental effect on them. Sometimes one meets individuals in counselling who have the most manifest psychological and emotional difficulties in their relationships at work, with partners and with their children. Such people may maintain an illusion that their childhoods were happy and satisfying, often in the face of clearly contradictory evidence. Or they may reason that their treatment as a child had nothing to do with their present day troubles which instead are presented as the fault of others - spouse, child, boss etc. They maintain a powerful victim stance, with the source of their persecution being displaced and diffused away from the past onto others in their daily lives.

Alternatively, denial and rationalisation may be so massive that the abuse in childhood is perceived as having been positive and 'character forming'. Sometimes such personalities become established in authoritarian occupations and hierarchical organisations which give opportunities for socially sanctioned exertions of aggressive authority, control and power. Denial and rationalisation are often the cornerstones of precariously established senses of identity and self-worth. In counselling these issues need to be addressed with gentleness and care, as there is the potential for sudden collapse into a primitive despair which can underlie such compensatory character formations. The power of these defences and family injunctions may linger for decades after the person has left the environment within which they were acquired - in this sense they have a timeless quality.

Splitting

From a very early age the potential for splitting between aspects of the child's developing personality become heightened. We have already discussed how, on an emotional level, aspects of the personality can start to become 'out of sync' through pseudo-maturity or emotional retardation. Such processes may be aggravated in the cognitive areas of development, creating disjointing and splitting within the crucial personality areas of self-image and identity.

The cognitive development of chronically abused children may adapt to mirror splitting and fragmentation in the personalities and relationships of the significant others around them: for example, a parent may appear as an entirely different personality when abusing the child and when not. This may have a nightmare quality for the child, e.g. the 'day time' father may be proud and loving, showing off his 'perfect angel' to all and sundry. Yet at night time, whilst abusing her, he may be menacing and threatening, projecting very different messages that she is a 'slut' and a 'whore'. Next morning, at breakfast, he is again as nice as pie. Such experiences have a potentially devastating impact. The sense of unreality and the experience of the parent as *two disconnected people* is incorporated into the child's experience of herself. In the above example, the child may adapt by developing a day time persona of 'angel' and a night time identity as 'slut'. In chronic abusive environments many other similar adaptive identities may develop at the cost of the establishment of an authentic and integrated personality.

Splitting is enhanced by the significance of denial. At both an individual psychological level and throughout the working of the family system, the perpetration of the abuse depends on a collusive denial that it is occurring at all. To outsiders, such families may appear to be normal, happy, even pillars of the community; and are related to as such. This augments the discrepancy for the child between the public pretence and the private reality.

These events contribute towards the experience of self as being a collection of fragmented and disconnected parts with little sense of a whole, integrated personality. To a degree this is a normal aspect of human experience and we habitually refer to ourselves in parts. However this can also become disabling: there may be experience of several parts of oneself with distinct voices, attitudes and roles; and commonly there are internal conversations, 'self-talk', arguments, self-commentating and sometimes noisy distracting babble. Such 'voices' often powerfully and critically repeat the original abusing family injunctions such as *'Don't trust... Don't tell...'* This constant repetition of self-defeating self-talk is invariably *anti-change* and *anti-therapy*.

'Parts' also may include child parts of the adult at different ages and clients will often already have their own descriptive labels or pet names: e.g. 'the child within'... the 'lost child'... 'my little boy'... 'little Janet'... etc. It can be helpful in therapy, at an appropriate time, to enquire about such experiences, as they are often not volunteered. The person may be cautious about this through fears of being or going crazy, or being seen as such. Therapeutically it is important to be able to identify 'key parts' and to be able to make contact with them. Careful attention to a sudden change in mood, body-posture, facial movements and tone of voice are often useful clues that something significant is happening. Asking simple questions such as *'What's happening now?'* or *'How old do you feel at the moment?'*, can lead into important emotional contact with repressed child parts of the personality. At such times therapeutic work involving enactment or visualisation can be very effective in 'letting go' of unresolved traumatic images and in 'resolving' such unfinished business in more satisfying ways from the standpoint of an empowered inner child.

Dissociative responses and post-traumatic stress disorder
The official psychiatric reference manual DSM-111-R [6] uses the following definitions:

> *'Dissociative Disorders: a disturbance or alteration in the normally integrative functions of identity, memory or consciousness. The disturbance or alteration may be sudden or gradual and transient or chronic.'*

> *'Post-Traumatic Stress Disorder: The essential feature of this disorder is the development of characteristic symptoms following a psychologically distressing event that is outside the range of usual human experience...the characteristic symptoms involve re-experiencing the traumatic event, avoidance of stimuli associated with the event or numbing of general responsiveness and increased arousal...The traumatic event can be re-experienced in a variety of ways. Commonly the person has recurrent and intrusive recollections of the event or recurrent distressing dreams during which the event is re-experienced.'*

These reactions are now well reported in research with adults who were abused as children [7] and a significant aspect of recovery may involve specific therapeutic work on alleviating these disabling difficulties. The following experiences are frequently reported: memory gaps (psychogenic amnesia), alterations in states of consciousness, aversion to or avoidance of certain situations, and the separation of self from body - out of body experiences. It is of note that psychiatric medication has no effective role in this area [8].

Memory gaps
Adults abused as children often report that there are parts of their childhood that they can remember nothing or very little about. Whole

chunks of early life have been repressed. Others may report that they have a fairly good recall of childhood in general, apart from some of the unknown abusive experiences. Still others have a vivid recall of abuse in detail, yet feel totally emotionally disconnected from the events, experiencing them as if watching a film. Invariably in counselling, memories of abuse are going to return and feelings are going to become *re-associated* - and this can be one of the most painful areas of work.

It is useful to establish an initial view as to the extent to which memory and feeling connection exists for the abusive events. Where there are reported large general memory gaps about whole periods of childhood, it is wise to assume that there may be major repression of chronic abuse. Therapy will need to proceed carefully, otherwise there is a danger of the client becoming overwhelmed by a sudden torrent of memories returning to consciousness.

Alterations in states of consciousness
There are several ways in which adults who were abused as children spontaneously experience these reactions in their daily lives. In essence this involves the induction of involuntary trance states [9]. The emotional intensity of the therapeutic setting is likely to provoke such experiences, thus creating the valuable opportunity for clients to work on recognition and management of their dissociative reactions directly in sessions. Briere [10] has described in detail common dissociative reactions experienced by adults who were abused as children. These include:

Disengagement: involves the cognitive separation of the individual from the environment at times of tension or stress. In a mild and transient form this is probably a common experience for most people. For example, the phenomena of day-dreaming and 'auto-piloting' in which only a portion of conscious attention is devoted to the task in hand whilst the predominant degree of conscious awareness is focussed elsewhere. To the extent that this enables repetitive tasks to be accomplished whilst mentally working on other problems, or relaxing, this is a productive allocation of selective attention. However, attention to the routine task can easily and unnoticeably become too minimal and this can affect performance and safety.

More severe and profound disengagement experiences attract metaphors such as 'spacing out', 'losing time' and 'shutting down'. Such reactions involve being triggered into an intense state of internal preoccupation, where immediate contact with and response to the environment is significantly reduced. Characteristically this often involves fixated eye focussing (a blank unresponsive look), stereotypical hand or finger movements (e.g. repetitive picking at clothing or pinching of skin), shallow breathing and non-response to verbal or physical contact. On the relatively infrequent occasions in which clients may regress to such out of contact trance states in sessions with little visible warning, counsellors may feel alarmed and inadequate with regard to knowing how to facilitate their return into contact with reality (see page 29).

Observing and spectatoring: This is another experience of separation from self involving the constant sense of *observing oneself in action* from a detached perspective, as opposed to being wholly and unselfconsciously present. It is often associated with an ongoing internal critical self-commentary and is highly likely to be present during sexual activity and thus a contributory factor to the sexual consequences of abuse. This experience of detachment and observation of self serves to diminish spontaneity in action and relationships and the quality and authenticity of contact with people.

Flashbacks: are a very commonly reported experience of adults who were abused as children. They often occur during sex where the client may suddenly re-experience the childhood abuse. Sometimes, in the course of this disorientation, the partner may be misperceived as the original abuser. Flashbacks are often triggered by known factors which have specific associations with the original abuse and commonly these are identifiable sexual actions which the victim wishes to avoid. However, triggers are by no means restricted to sexual matters - *anything* relating to the circumstances of the original trauma may provoke this reaction. Clients have spoken in bewilderment of flashbacks occurring in response to the smell of burning toast and of hearing a baby cry in the street.

What is less often volunteered, however, is that flashbacks may be regularly occurring in all sorts of situations without particular triggers that the person can recognise or identify. Again, the reticence in volunteering this may be connected with fears of madness. Therapeutic work will involve helping the client to begin to identify their own particular trigger associations, perhaps to explore their original source (i.e. the significance of burning toast to the experience of being abused) and to practise techniques for avoidance and de-sensitisation of the triggers as well as 'grounding' techniques (see page 29) to bring a dissociative episode to an end. The therapeutic task is to enable the client to learn how to bring such involuntary experiences under conscious ego control. This is an area of work where rapid progress is often possible and where the increased confidence gained as a result spins over positively into other areas of life.

Nightmares: Sleep disturbances involving nightmares are common. The content often involves re-enactment of the abuse in some form, experiences of victimisation and powerlessness and perhaps sadistic retaliatory images. Encouraging clients to share the content of nightmares in sessions, facilitating the exploration - and really testing - of feelings of powerlessness and fantasies of revenge, often gradually takes the pressure off the frequency and intensity of nightmares, as their unconscious content is increasingly expressed through a conscious inter-personal relationship with the therapist. When phases of nightmares recur during therapy, they are sometimes the precursor of the return of further repressed abuse material into consciousness.

Out of Body Experiences: Many victims describe a profound dissociative defence acquired during the act of abuse - that of a separation of mind from body. The mind leaves the body behind to the mercy of the abuser and takes itself away 'To a Safer Place'. During therapy, victims may symbolically or actually return to the scene of the abuse to 'reclaim' their lost child part which was split off and left behind [11].

Dissociative reactions such as these should be considered with all adults who were abused as children and who are seeking counselling and therapy. Clients usually have a welcome sense of relief when the counsellor shows an awareness of such phenomena and can relate these to the similar experiences of others. Knowledge that the symptoms are not unique can gradually take the pressure off the awful internal fear of being crazy. It is essential that such exploration is done in a way which is reassuring to the client. Fortunately, many schools of modern psychotherapy have normalised notions of segments of the personality, developing from Freud's own 'parts' model of the psyche (the id, ego and super-ego) and the conflicts between them. Concepts drawn from Transactional Analysis (the parent, adult and child ego states) and the notion from psychosynthesis of *sub-personalities* are very helpful in this respect [12, 13, 14].

Social Consequences

A major difficulty for adults who were abused as children is often that of achieving and maintaining intimacy in personal relationships. There may be a fear of intimacy: a fear of being known, being rejected and a fear of being perceived as bad, even for victims who have established apparently successful lives and careers. This may be compounded by an uncertain sense of personal identity, experience of de-personalisation and a pre-occupation with existential questions such as 'Who am I?' There may be a pervasive sense of unreality about the self and the world. At the extreme, 'being real' may only be felt in the role and experience of being abused and experiencing pain. This may contribute to masochistic and destructive tendencies which can underlie the familiar pattern of continuing victimisation in adulthood.

The combination of over-adaptability to the needs of others and poorly developed sense of personal identity may show through shallowness in relationships or in a manner of detachment. A common metaphor is of 'The Wall' which prevents others getting close enough to recognise one's vulnerability and simultaneously inhibits spontaneous contact and responses towards others. On occasions such needs may erupt and the adult abused as a child may latch onto another in a demanding and dependent fashion, in all likelihood scaring the person away by the sheer intensity of need. These patterns repeat and become self-reinforcing. Consequently the pain of loneliness and isolation, regardless of how many people are encountered, is often chronic.

When relationships occur certain difficulties tend to predominate. The insecurity generated by unmet childhood dependency needs, and damage to basic trust, often leads to constant testing of partners and the provocation of rejection. There may be difficulties in accepting and giving physical affection and serious problems around conflict resolution in relationships. Conflict may be desperately avoided, or it may be compulsively provoked. Sometimes marriages or commitments are formed on the basis of a flight from the original abusive environment, or impulsively with the first available person, as an escape from loneliness. Such relationships, which often involve the unconscious attraction of two equally deprived personalities, may be precipitously formed on the basis of intense, immature and unrealistic expectations that - at long last - someone has been found who can meet all of their unmet needs. In such scenarios, the magical fantasy inevitably is soon dispelled and can result in a spiral of mounting frustration, mutual bitterness and provocation, which can escalate into serious violence.

Other relationships may be formed on the basis of one partner taking the role of 'rescuer' to the other. However, the depth of emotional need is often so great that it proves impossible for any one person to meet. Eventually the repressed needs of the rescuer may burst to the surface and the switch can be made into a rejecting and persecutory position. The dynamics between the positions of victim, rescuer and persecutor described by Karpman as the *'Drama Triangle'* are highly relevant in the social relationships of many adults who were abused as children[15]. The search for intimacy has many pitfalls and is likely to be one of the major areas addressed during therapeutic work. This begins with the experiential learning opportunity which is presented by the special form of intimacy developed in the relationship with the counsellor.

Common socially adaptive patterns

Eliana Gil [16] has described three broad typical ways in which adults who were abused as children develop patterns of dealing with the world: *Acting-out, Accommodating* and *Helping*. It can be useful to have in mind the general features of each type of reaction:

Acting out: is characterised by destructive, self-destructive, abusive, self-abusive and risk-taking behaviour. This can involve criminal activities, drug and alcohol abuse, promiscuity and prostitution etc. Self-hatred with masochistic undertones is common, as are feelings of worthlessness and dependence on the sexual use of the body as the main form of human contact. Acting-out, often with risk-taking and aggressive behaviour, may be overall more characteristic of abused males than females. The female propensity to 'act-in' emotional problems, in comparison to males who 'act-out', leads to a diversion in social responses whereby in general women are dealt with by mental health systems and males by criminal justice systems. However, some women do act-out in response to histories of serious and chronic abuse, especially when in their teens and twenties. At this time they are often highly resistant to therapeutic help.

Counsellors are often approached by mainstream agencies to offer help to such adolescents and young adults. Unfortunately, it is rare that people in 'acting-out mode' can settle sufficiently into a structure and continuity which is necessary for effective counselling. This can be a great frustration to referrers whose own anxiety is often the pressing issue rather than the needs felt by the client at that point. Often the best the counsellor can achieve is to have a satisfactory single session using skills of listening and empathy to communicate to the person concerned that help will be available if and when they themselves decide that the time is right.

The prognosis for 'acting-out' adults abused as children, especially females, in the long-term is not necessarily poor. If the angry and destructive energy can gradually be re-channelled into constructive and creative directions - and maturation often helps this along - then significant positive changes can occur. At least the anger is near to the surface and accessible and therefore open to direct therapeutic work. This is not so with the other two types of response.

'Accommodators': Accommodators experience profound early damage and the core of their problem is a lack of a sense of inner self. Accommodators learn to live in roles, adapting each persona subtly to the needs of each other person or situation they are in. It is difficult to get any sense of the real person behind the roles, or the masks, apart from the need to please or to be perfect, or to avoid conflict or rejection. They present a particularly difficult therapeutic challenge for the counsellor to get anywhere near to the real feelings of vulnerability and anger, beneath what is often a rather 'immaculate' exterior. The counsellor needs to be aware that people who have been damaged in this way can also adapt to the role of 'client' and behave in ways to 'please' the therapist. Sometimes illusions of progress can be made which are artificial and inauthentic and therapists pleased with their own 'success' may not be alert to this.

'Helpers': It is known that abused people are over-represented in the various 'helping' professions. Many readers of this book will themselves have been abused and many more will have suffered degrees of emotional deprivation. Abused people can and do make excellent therapists and counsellors. However, to achieve this it is vital that they have sufficiently worked with their own experience and reactions to being abused so that their own 'business' can be kept predominantly separate from that of their clients. This is unlikely to occur unless the person has received the benefit of their own abuse-related counselling or therapy.

Sexual consequences

Research and reports from practice consistently show that high proportions of adults who were abused as children experience sexual problems of one kind or another. Commonly reported difficulties include:
• suppression of sexual awareness, desire and responsiveness
• promiscuous or compulsive sexual activity
• difficulties with orgasm, vaginismus
• damaging and distressing association of sexual arousal with specific

stimuli such as pain/anger or strangers
- disturbing sexual fantasies including fantasies of abusing
- flashbacks and other dissociative responses during sexual activity
- confusion re sexual identity and orientation
- fear of vulnerability associated with sexual arousal and loss of control.

Sex therapists often report that sexual problems in general tend to resolve once the underlying relationship problems are effectively dealt with. This maxim seems highly appropriate to work with adults who were abused as children. The variety of consequences described so far are all likely to interfere in a number of ways with the establishment and maintenance of satisfying sexual relationships. Progress towards remedying these will enable clients gradually to gain confidence in tackling sexual problems which remain, as satisfactions in other areas of life develop. For this reason work on sexual difficulties is likely to occur towards the end of abuse-related therapy [17].

Males

Research generated by the increase in awareness in recent years regarding the effects in adult life of childhood abuse has focussed predominantly on females who were sexually abused as children by men. The propensity and role of women as sexual abusers is only now just beginning to be talked about, although experienced practitioners often encounter reports of such abuse from male and female clients alike. Less research has been undertaken with regard to any significant differences between the genders relating to the long term effects of abuse. Clinical experience suggests that whilst in general men may be less likely to perceive abuse as having been damaging and are less likely to seek - and to find - therapeutic help; that when they do so, many of the key issues relating to consequences and recovery are very similar for both sexes.

Men may be reluctant to disclose abuse histories for a number of reasons. It does not match stereotypical notions of male roles in society and there may be fears of being perceived as having 'female' traits such as helplessness, submissiveness and passivity. Such victim attributes are less congruent with social perceptions of masculinity than they are with social perceptions of femininity and as such may create greater anxiety and consequent concealment in males. For males sexually abused by men, intense anxieties relating to sexual identity may be present. There may be a phase of confused sexual orientation, fears of becoming homosexual, being perceived as homosexual, confusing one's natural gay orientation with the abuse, or having others construe it in such a way.

Culturally, men are inclined to see sex in terms of how easy or difficult it is to get, rather than whether it was a good or a damaging experience. With regard to abuse of boys by women, peer group responses are likely to perceive such events as having been 'lucky'. In situations such as premature sexual initiation by a woman, and even in cases of painful abuse by a male, the male victim may fail to develop any awareness that the experience might in some way have been harmful. Indeed it is not uncommon for men to interpret such events as having been 'character forming', which in turn can provide a significant ingredient of a later potential rationalisation for inflicting the same abuse on somebody else.

Common sexual dysfunctions for abused males include avoidance of sex, performance difficulties, acting-out and sexual compulsions or addictions. Withdrawal and aversion to sex may be a dynamic behind a decision to lead a life of celibacy. Male abuse victims are far more likely to have problems than non-abused men in achieving and maintaining an erection, premature ejaculation, difficulty in ejaculating, together with low sexual desire and arousal. There may be significant performance anxieties associated with these difficulties which reinforce and compound them. Such anxiety may also contribute to insecurity and jealousy, which may become pathological.

Acting-out reactions, especially for abused adolescent and young adult males, tend to involve either the rejection of maleness or the flaunting of maleness. The former may involve identification with homosexual culture and may include prostitution. The latter may involve an identification with gangs or hyper-macho heroes such as *Rambo*, including homophobic traits which at the extreme may be acted out through abusive behaviour such as 'queer bashing'.

The acting out of heterosexual abused males often includes a dominant view of male sexuality which sees females as possessions and objects and with whom sexual arousal is associated with exertion of power. Emotional dependence on the woman is denied although this may be clearly recognisable through over-controlling behaviour and pathological jealousy. Males who were sexually abused by women, who take this 'macho' acting-out route, may have a strong association of sexual arousal with fantasies, or acts, of violence towards women. A certain category of rapists - so called 'revenge rapists' - are an extreme example of this. If their own abuse by a woman involved aspects of humiliation, the consequent rage may include contempt of female sexual arousal and the perceived demands or sexual hunger of women.

Sexual compulsions and 'addictions', whilst a possible consequence for both genders, may have specific masculine forms of expression usually connected with aggression. Hypersexuality - an abnormally high and powerful sex drive - can be quickly destructive of relationships. The re-enactment compulsion can contribute to the progression of a proportion of males who were abused as children who go on to become abusers. Currently it is not clearly understood precisely which categories of abused males go on to abuse children and what are the precise dynamics which result in such behaviour. Synthesis of the available research suggests that about one-third of sexually abused males will at some time abuse a child (not necessarily their own) and that two-thirds will not [18]. There is no evidence which suggests that either a heterosexual or a homosexual orientation constitutes a greater predisposing factor to abuse children.

Retrospectively, it is known that very high proportions, around 70-90%, of established male child sexual abusers were themselves abused when they were children. However, it is important not to misconstrue this consistent finding: it does *not* mean that 70-90% of abused males will go on to become abusers.

Beginning Abuse-Related Counselling

The description of therapeutic issues which follows reflects counselling practice in which help has been specifically sought for abuse-related problems. However, all counsellors will continue to come across childhood abuse in the course of ongoing work with some clients who initially came for other reasons. In such situations, if both the counsellor and client are able to recognise that abuse issues lie at the core of the problem, then the focus can be adjusted onto abuse-related work which may then follow the sorts of directions we are about to discuss.

Initial sessions

Boundaries: The introductory session, or sometimes the first couple of sessions, may most usefully be used for developing an initial impression of the following key areas: the specific nature of the client's difficulties, including whether or not there is a current crisis; expectations of counselling; and previous experiences of counselling. The counsellor, bearing these issues in mind, can also provide information about the service available. It is rarely helpful, and often counter-productive, for clients to use initial sessions to talk in detail about the abuse. The most important purpose of initial sessions is to establish rapport and to agree the context and boundaries of the counselling - to establish the prospect of, and ground-rules for, the *'safe container'* of the working relationship, rather than to dive unprepared into abuse-related material.

Sometimes clients who 'splurge' a lot of abuse-related material in first sessions do not subsequently return. This can leave the counsellor feeling 'dumped on' with a pile of unpleasant and often distressing material, even themselves feeling somewhat abused by the experience. Clients who behave in this way may be acting-out their process regarding lack of consistent boundaries - sometimes with an unconscious undercurrent of aggression and persecution - directed at the unsuspecting counsellor. They may have a history of similar single sessions with a number of previous counsellors or agencies. The failure to return exemplifies some of the issues we have described, including anxiety regarding the possibility of intimacy, shame, unconscious aggression and chaos or inconsistency in emotional life and social relationships.

If such 'splurging' seems about to occur in initial sessions, it can be very helpful to comment gently but firmly that one does not feel that the time is quite right for the abuse to be discussed in detail until the nature of the counselling relationship has been agreed. Such a response provides an important intervention into the crucial area of the client's experience and utilisation of inappropriate boundaries. Initial sessions which incorporate attention to boundaries, with the counsellor commenting on and modelling appropriate and clear ones, lay the necessary foundation for abuse-related matters to be productively addressed throughout the therapy. Without such a foundation, the therapeutic house is likely to fall down during stormy periods of testing out by the client; or an unconscious collusion between counsellor and client to avoid potentially difficult material may develop.

Developing rapport: Initial sessions are also key moments which affect the establishment of rapport and the potential working alliance, and this can be crucial to the decision of the client whether or not to continue. It can be useful to acknowledge one's own anxiety about meeting a new person for the first time and to share one's sense that the client may be feeling very anxious - if not absolutely terrified - about the encounter. If this promotes a knowing response, engagement can be facilitated by exploring how that anxiety is being experienced in the moment.

Exploring *ambivalence* about attending the initial session will often provide information, and a sense of relief, that such anxieties are common and understandable. This ambivalence may involve an acute approach-avoidance dilemma: one client described how she had set out very early for her appointment, had sat across the road in a cafe watching the building for a period of time, had then approached the door and gone past it on three occasions before finally plucking up the courage to go inside! Acknowledging such 'here and now' anxieties at the beginning of the initial session serves to alleviate them somewhat and contributes to the development of rapport. However there are several other areas which repay early exploration in initial sessions affecting the clarification of boundaries and the establishment of rapport:

Why has the referral been made? By whom? And why now? What is the significance in the client's life, when the abuse may have taken place many years ago, that help is being sought at this moment? *The dynamics of the referral may provide very significant information about the abuse-related processes of the client and the impact of these on relationships.* Is the referral the result of a crisis? If so, is it predominantly an internal emotional/psychological crisis or is it a relationship crisis? For the former, is the crisis still current and acute? And if so is the client's immediate need for support and containment and is this recognised? People may be referred who are in such a state of crisis that they feel they are falling apart or becoming 'unglued', and occasionally there may be clear signs of a significant psychiatric disturbance. **This is not a good time to focus in therapy specifically on the abuse issues,** although the counsellor may well offer a supportive role orientated around containment. In such situations suicidal thoughts are common and a psychiatric assessment of the client is often advisable. This serves both the interests of the client and the security of the counsellor.

Sometimes people are referred under degrees of pressure from significant others. Identifying this can go a long way towards understanding a sense of withdrawal or passive hostility in the client's manner. A typical scenario is where someone has been issued with an ultimatum by a partner to *'go and get yourself sorted out or I'm leaving...'* In such cases, the crisis predominantly lies within the relationship, although this may have been triggered by, or may precipitate, an emotional 'caving in' on the part of the individual. Other people may be referred or may refer themselves because of a growing awareness that many of the difficulties they have faced in life and relationships are ultimately connected with their abusive experiences as children. They may have known for a long time of the need for help before arriving at a point in their lives where the 'time is now right'. This often seems to happen to people in their thirties and forties. Such referrals are usually not crisis led and the therapeutic outcome is likely to be particularly good.

Availability of family and community support: If people are referred in a state of crisis the degree of outside support will be an immediately pressing concern. The involvement of significant others in the management of the crisis is likely to be an early focus of attention. Because of the very nature of the abuse-history, commonly there is no, or little, prospect of any appropriate, realistic or consistent support from within the family of origin. However there may be exceptions to this which can be usefully identified.

If the client has a partner, his or her attitudes will be crucial. This is so whether or not the work is beginning from a point of crisis. Crisis or not, if there is a partner it can be helpful to invite that person along to participate in an early joint session. The partner will undoubtedly have his or her own anxieties about the counselling, along with fantasies and possibly unrealistic expectations as to what this will involve. The ability and inclination of partners to be consistently supportive, understanding and patient, may be enhanced by an initial personal contact with the counsellor and by being given information which enables them to understand and anticipate some of the themes and difficulties which may arise as the work progresses.

A crucial part of the information giving, both individually with the client and with the partner if possible, is that *things tend to get worse before they get better* and that recovery and growth involves a painful and bumpy passage along an unpredictable road which has many diversions and pitfalls. For example, as work progresses new memories tend to return and feelings can be experienced and expressed in more intense and volatile ways. This can be de-stabilising and frightening, although therapeutically inevitable. At such times, adults who were abused as children can be particularly difficult to live with. **If the relationship with the partner at the point of referral is not in crisis, it is likely to be so at some point during the therapeutic work.** Partners need warning about this prospect in the hope of minimising an understandable but unfortunate reaction which is to say 'Counselling is making you worse, not better...' and putting pressure on the client to withdraw. The needs of partners for their own support is often very apparent. The offer of separate individual counselling (with another counsellor) and/or joint sessions may be necessary and appropriate.

It is helpful to be aware of other actual and potential supports within the community. The need for, and difficulties in, asking for support is likely to be an important theme in the client's life. Low self esteem and poor self image inhibit use of potential social supports. The availability of a therapeutic group for adults abused as children, through the combination of therapeutic work and peer support, can make an enormous contribution to confidence, healing and growth [19].

What does the client understand about the counselling process? What has s/he been told by the referrer?

Exploring perceptions and fantasies about what getting help may involve will also contribute important knowledge for the counsellor as to clients' current views of themselves and their worlds. It is helpful to be able to form an initial impression of the degree of realism of expectations of the help on offer and to clarify these as appropriate by providing accurate information. Many clients build themselves up into states of acute anxiety whilst awaiting the initial appointment by assuming (or having been told) that they will be expected to talk all about the gory details of the abuse in the very first session to a total stranger. Indeed, this may be why some highly anxious clients 'splurge' in the first session - having psyched themselves up to blurt it all out.

Such exploration offers an early opportunity for the counsellor to explain his or her ways of working and to give realistic information about the prospective therapeutic journey ahead. Clients often ask *'How long will it take?'* It is important to give realistic answers about timescales and to avoid false reassurance. The only really honest reply is to say *'I don't know, but I'm willing to work with you to help you find out...'* In my experience the general range of time people spend in abuse-related counselling at any one time is between three months and four years. However, recovery as a whole may involve a number of different phases of therapy at different times, with important breaks in between. It should not be allowed to become a compulsive process: all the work does not have to be done at one time!

To be clearer about timescales and for the client and counsellor to form a sense as to whether they will feel comfortable working together, it can be helpful to agree a set number of sessions - six seems to be a useful number - and then to review progress. If it is decided that work should proceed further this can be on an open ended basis or according to another renewable set period of time. An issue arises with regard to private fee-paying clients in contrast to agency clients who receive a free service. My sense is that some clients who receive a free service over a long period of time do not experience the therapeutically beneficial effect of making a financial investment in the process which matches the skills/experience commitment of the counsellor. In periods where work is slow, or even stuck, counsellors in such situations are unable to focus clients on the question as to whether or not they feel they are getting value for money from the process and their own contribution to it. Without a noticeable yet affordable financial investment, for some clients the work may tend to be slower and achieve less. In such circumstances this can best be addressed by using renewable, time limited contracts, which maintain the best possible level of attention focussed on the value of what is being undertaken.

This is a matter concerning therapeutic effectiveness, not an argument in itself for such counselling only to be provided within private fee-paying relationships. Many adults who were abused as children do not have the financial resources to pay for private therapy and there is a clear need for effective therapeutic services to be developed by statutory and voluntary agencies.

Exploration of previous therapeutic histories
Many clients will have received various forms of help in the past from

other counsellors and agencies. These experiences can powerfully affect perceptions and expectations of the new relationship. Again, exploration of this in the initial sessions can lead to valuable information regarding the prospect of transference issues lingering from previous helpers. Such histories have potentially powerful implications, as feelings and themes stemming from experiences with previous counsellors will inevitably, consciously or unconsciously, be projected onto the new relationship. For example, a client may feel that he or she was 'abandoned' by a past 'good' therapist and may consequently inhibit investment in the new relationship for fear that this may recur. Alternatively, and perhaps more commonly, clients may report a wide range of negative feelings about previous helpers. It is not unusual for clients to have had relationships with several professionals without being able to reveal or talk about their abuse [20]. They may feel that such people were unable or unwilling to listen or to respond appropriately. Others have felt that professionals were personally uncomfortable with the abuse material, giving impressions of wishing to avoid or minimise it. On the other hand, some clients have felt uncomfortable with what they perceived as a prurient interest in the details of the abuse and, even more damagingly, the vulnerability of some clients to being sexually exploited by professionals under the guise of 'counselling' is being increasingly reported [21].

If issues such as these are identified, it is helpful for the effective development of the potential new therapeutic relationship that the boundary issues which arise can be addressed and clarified at an early stage. Whatever the content of the client's previous unsatisfactory experiences, the implicit question will always be present: *'Will it happen here too?'* This area of counselling invariably has at the heart of the process work which relates to boundary disturbances. Clients bring a history of such infringements to sessions and may consciously or unconsciously look to re-establish or re-play these within the new relationship, at the same time testing out the counsellor's willingness for this to happen.

Many of these points are identical to work with non-abused clients, although their actual or symbolic significance may be greater. Arrangements regarding length and frequency of sessions should be kept to from the beginning, as testing-out by the client, particularly at times of crisis, may lead the counsellor into an anxious reaction of over-extending sessions, or of being immediately available at other times. Whilst this may feel a 'caring' thing to do and on one level be perceived by the client as such, it can be counter-productive. When such pressures occur it is very important that the underlying *process* is explored and that the counsellor is clear whether or not such a response is helpful or whether it is in fact an avoidance of another response which ultimately might be more therapeutically beneficial.

Agreement needs to be reached at the beginning of work regarding the *out of session availability of the counsellor*. If counsellors are unclear about their own boundaries, very needy and demanding clients can significantly impinge on their other work space and private time which, when occurring, can be far harder to stop than to prevent. Agency counsellors who give their home telephone numbers to clients or private counsellors who do not have clear limits about out-of-session contact can find themselves feeling very intruded upon and abused by the type and extent of demands which may be made. *This is a significant expression of the client's testing-out process* which, as we have already noted, is likely to be a major theme in the therapy.

Clients working on these themes will unconsciously push until they meet firmness. Continual flexibility and 'giving' by the counsellor does not meet this need and is therapeutically counter-productive. It is also unhealthy for the counsellor who inevitably, consciously or unconsciously, begins to experience negative counter-transference feelings towards the client. Concealed resentment at facing unreasonable demands often has significant historical personal importance for counsellors who operate with loose boundaries. The stage can become set for a variation of the classic Karpman triangle switch which results in the counsellor coming to experience himself/herself as *victim of the persecutory client*.

This is a description of a fairly extreme but not uncommon scenario for helping professionals. It highlights the importance of early awareness of boundary issues and the need to promote explicit exploration of these in sessions rather than to become seduced into a process of acceding to superficially innocuous requests. Apparently trivial events may contain the most profound unconscious meaning and communication. Being alert to such content and being willing to pay detailed attention to it offers a potent opportunity for exploration within the therapeutic relationship which can significantly shorten the period of time that might otherwise be required to get to the core themes of the client's problems. It is in this area that Gestalt therapy and familiarity with writers such as Langs [22], Cashdan [23], Casement [24] and Storr [25] on unconscious communication within the transference and counter-transference relationship can be especially valuable and effective.

Unconscious questioning or comment on the therapeutic relationship may become manifest in many subtle ways. For example, punctuality, regularity and time-keeping: what is the message within incidents or patterns of being late, early or even consistently exactly on time for sessions? What is the real message behind a missed session? Does the client watch the clock or ignore it? Does the client regularly bring up key material at the end of sessions - preventing its exploration or alluring the counsellor into extending the session? Be aware of the very first and very last things said in each session (so-called 'door knob' comments) as these often have special significance as unconscious commentary on the therapeutic relationship.

Physical appearance and mannerisms are also powerful communication channels for unconscious material. The symbolic significance of the way people dress ranges from the almost imperceptible to the blatantly overt. No matter what the gender combination of counsellor and client, the client who regularly or suddenly appears in revealing attire is drawing attention to issues of sexuality within the transference relationship which can be very challenging to the counsellor - and thereby tempting but inexpedient to ignore.

Likewise, noticing subtle changes in attention, facial movements, body posture, tone and levels of voice; and commenting on these as they occur can facilitate the client's connection with cognitive and emotional reactions which are powerfully affecting the way they think, feel and behave at a subconscious level. Such changes can be indicative of dissociative responses and exploration of the client's sense of *'What is happening now?'* will often lead into important areas of inner life. For example, it is common to notice changes in voice tone and body postures which may assume a more child-like quality. Asking the question *'How old do you feel at this moment?'* may lead to answers which indicate that the person is very much in touch with an inner child experience which has a precise orientation in a specific time and age. Encouraging the client to give voice to this 'child-part' of themselves and to describe where they are and what is happening around them in this experience, can be a profound part of therapy. Such exploration often facilitates the return to conscious awareness of important repressed memories.

Such regressive work should only be undertaken by counsellors and therapists who have some training and experience in this form of therapy. It is important to test and establish beforehand that clients who have the inclination to work regressively also have the ability and motivation to 'return' to present day reality - and to get on with their daily lives at the end of the therapeutic session. Clients with histories of borderline connections with reality are, initially at least, more likely to benefit from work which enhances their ability to *stay* in the 'here and now' rather than slipping habitually into some form of altered state in sessions.

'Grounding' techniques are effective in assisting the client to keep in touch with or return to the 'here and now' reality. They include: inviting the client to pay conscious attention to their breathing e.g. to breathe more regularly and deeply as breathing often becomes slower and fainter during dissociative experiences or emotional arousal; requesting that the client resumes eye-contact whilst reminding the client of where they are, what day it is, where they have come from before the session and where they will be going to afterwards and asking the client to elaborate on this; requesting clients to place their feet firmly on the floor, to experience the solidity of this and to look around the room recognising all of the familiar surroundings. As contact resumes - occasionally the counsellor may have to be quite firm about some of these methods - it can be helpful to provide an explanation for the experience they have just had and reassurance that they are safe and in control.

Planned regressive work often starts with suggestions from the counsellor that the client begins to relax, breathes more deeply and allows their attention to gradually shift away from external preoccupations and onto sensations and images which may begin to appear from within. It is effective at the same time to suggest to the client that during this experience a part of their attention will remain attentive to the therapist's voice and that they will return into contact with the therapist when this suggestion is made. Also, during the experience, they will continue to report to the therapist 'what is happening'.

For some clients, regressive work can be extremely powerful and healing; facilitating through enactment or imagery the re-solving in more satisfactory ways traumatic events of the past. Therapists who work in such ways appreciate the importance of graduating the depth of exploration and keeping an adult to adult connection with the client throughout the experience so that the therapist can quickly and safely lead the client 'back' to present day reality at an appropriate moment. Reflecting on such experiences and integrating the meaning and learning derived from them is as important as the experience itself. Always allow sufficient time at the end of sessions for 'processing' and reflecting on what has taken place!

Confidentiality

Finally, it is important that counsellors and clients are clear about *confidentiality - and exceptions to it.* Discussing this can address some key concerns about trust and containment. Two appropriate confidentiality exceptions are: any knowledge of ongoing child abuse within the family or any serious concerns felt by the counsellor about the client's mental state, particularly risk of suicide.

Child abuse: A client may be concerned that the person who abused them is currently abusing other children. These may be younger siblings, grandchildren, nieces or nephews; or children in other contexts - including children seen by the abuser within a professional or social role. Before clients reveal such information in detail it is important that they are aware of the counsellor's wider responsibilities which, for counsellors working in agency settings, will be outlined in some form of policy and procedural manual. If action to protect children who are currently being abused is initiated by a counsellor on the basis of information provided in a therapeutic context without the client expecting this, the effect on the client and the therapeutic relationship can be disastrous. The damage involves betrayal of trust, loss of control and the provocation of destructive reverberations within the extended family which could potentially place the client in danger.

However, when appropriate, if such matters are raised at the beginning of work, most clients express understanding and acceptance of the purpose and need for this exception to confidentiality. Raising this at the outset allows such fears to be expressed and explored without a sense of loss of control. The client knows that unless he or she names the abuser or the child concerned then reporting the matter would not be possible. The primary focus then can be on ways in which the client feels he or she should act to protect the child and to work towards taking some personal responsibility for doing so with the counsellor's support rather than for the counsellor to deal with the matter on the client's behalf.

Another possible area of concern regarding child abuse arises in work with adults abused as children who have also abused children. Taking abuse to include physical and sexual abuse, this is equally likely to be a factor with both male and female clients. It is therapeutically vital - and a fundamental principle of the need to protect children - that counsellors do not get stuck in *'confidentiality traps'* involving knowledge of ongoing abusing behaviour. Clarity from the outset about this matter provides a necessary baseline of security for both counsellor and client.

It is both ethically and therapeutically wrong to continue work with clients who are abusing children without the involvement of child protection agencies. To do so promotes a relationship of collusion with the client which is interpreted as condoning their behaviour. This reinforces such clients' inner processes of denial, rationalisation and guilt-alleviation. The prime therapeutic need is for a boundary which requires that the abusive behaviour is stopped and for the therapeutic work only to proceed on that basis.

Mental health concerns and suicide risk: Sometimes during the therapeutic process, if not at the time of referral, a number of adults who were abused as children feel suicidal or fear that they may be 'going crazy'. It can be helpful and reassuring for this to be acknowledged at an early stage and a contingency response to be agreed should the need arise. As with the confidentiality exception for child abuse, it is rarely the case that clients are anything but accepting of the reasons for and the sense of this. Again, however, it is far more therapeutic to have raised the issue and developed an understanding about what this will involve *before* it happens than for the counsellor to have to suddenly behave in a way during a crisis that the client did not expect. It is preferable for the client himself or herself to agree to seek a psychiatric appointment via their own GP. On occasions it may be helpful for the counsellor to have obtained permission to discuss the relevant concerns with the GP and the psychiatrist. Only in rare situations would it be necessary to make such contacts without the current consent of the client.

Gently exploring confidentiality issues at the initial stage of therapy sometimes reveals the existence of current and historical fears in a very useful way. For example, many clients express strong feelings about psychiatrists and unfortunately for some these are based on the reality of previous unsatisfactory experiences. For others such feelings are to do with an ingrained belief that seeing a psychiatrist confirms one's worst fears about the inevitability of madness in the context of old messages within their families about 'being crazy' and 'needing to be locked up...'

Liaison with local psychiatric services is very valuable. A small number of clients will need psychiatric involvement during the course of their counselling. This is likely to be due to suicidal crises, self-harming behaviour, serious eating disorders, acute dissociative states or the establishment of a depth of depression which renders the person unable to cope with daily life and puts them beyond the reach of a communicative relationship. Given this and the common recovery process which invariably involves 'getting worse before better', liaison with local psychiatrists is also vital to help them avoid coming to the conclusion that all clients are being damaged by counselling!

The Therapeutic Journey

Throughout therapy with adults who were abused as children there are likely to be three major areas which are the focus of attention. These are: *The dynamics of the therapeutic relationship*, *Other significant relationships* and *Telling the Story*. Many clients will also need to work on a fourth: *Management of dissociative responses*, already discussed (page 29) but see also page 43.

1. The therapeutic relationship

We shall see later that a specific component of abuse-related therapy is the opportunity to 'tell the story' of the abuse to a significant other in a safe environment. The therapeutic relationship provides this environment but telling the story will only be helpful at a stage when this relationship, which contains the potential for powerful transference and counter-transference dynamics, is working openly and creatively.

Transference: Transference is a key notion in psychodynamic schools of psychotherapy and counselling and in fact is a universal human experience. Perceptions and attitudes regarding another person (or groups of people) are influenced and affected by previous contacts and relationships with significant other people - often parental and other authority figures - in the past. Therapy clearly (and in traditional analytic schools, deliberately) arouses such phenomena given the relatively helpless, childlike and vulnerable position of being a client, in contrast to the authority and parent-like role of therapist. Consequently, within a therapeutic relationship old patterns of perceiving and relating to others are likely to be consciously and unconsciously re-enacted with the therapist. This provides a powerful opportunity for the client to become more aware of such attitudes and behaviour and learn to relate gradually to the therapist as a real person rather than as a complex mixture of reality and representations of aspects of significant others.

Briere [26] described three overlapping domains of transference. Firstly, there are chronic distortions of adult inter-personal perceptions that reflect a 'world view' with events and relationships being interpreted through this distorting filter. For example: *'All men are bad... are only interested in sex...'* or *'No woman can be trusted...'* Such views powerfully influence in a negative way a person's ability and willingness to trust others. The second level involves more acute and immediate emotional reactions when some specific aspect of the interaction with another person re-stimulates childhood issues, particularly trauma. For example, some incident between the therapist and client may spark a strong emotional response which is essentially incongruent or disproportionate to the actual event. For example, a reassuringly offered touch may not be perceived as such - whatever the gender combination of therapist and client.

Thirdly, Briere described a level of transference involving *'sustained alterations in perception of the other derived from certain similarities and connections with psychologically important people in childhood.'* At this level the transference involves a reaction to certain characteristics of the counsellor or therapist - to factors such as age, appearance, culture, social class, intelligence, perceived attractiveness, profession and gender, etc. As an example of this, in one of our early groups for adults abused as children, a woman had a noticeable difficulty in relating to one of the group leaders who was a female doctor. In exploring this, we were able to discover the original transference basis: when the woman was a child she had been sexually abused by a number of men wearing white coats brought into her home by her mother who had told her they were doctors...

This level of transference relates to gender and questions often arise as to whether there is a 'right' or most therapeutically effective gender combination. For people who have been abused this has major transference possibilities. It is important to explore feelings about this at the beginning of work. In agency practice (where the client may have little choice as to the allocation of counsellors) it would be unhelpful and inappropriate to insist on a counsellor of a particular gender for an aversive client. On the relatively rare occasions that a potential client expresses a strong preference, it is important to respect this.

Transference themes and events
A common transference theme involves the client's unconscious expectation and fantasy that the counsellor will somehow become the yearned for 'good parent' who can and will meet all of their unmet emotional and dependency needs outstanding from childhood. The fact that no one person - not even a counsellor - can ever meet all of the emotional needs of another, particularly needs which stem from significant emotional deprivation, means that inevitably the therapeutic process is going to be an inherently frustrating experience for the client.

The counsellor who attentively resists accommodating to such transference expectations and demands will inevitably generate frustration for the client. The opportunity to reflect on and gradually become more aware of the meaning of this frustration in the context of a real relationship with another provides the therapeutic ingredient for the development of intimacy skills. However it is important to anticipate a possible counter-transference reaction on the part of the counsellor. If the transference demand by the client for the counsellor to become a substitute 'good parent' corresponds to the counsellor's own secret emotional agenda of 'nurturing' or 'rescuing' others, then the counsellor may be operating from the premise that he or she can provide exactly what the client is yearning for. Such transference/counter-transference collusion is set for disaster: crises are likely to occur as the client becomes increasingly demanding, the counsellor increasingly exhausted, in which ultimately the counsellor switches from the position of 'rescuer' of the client to that of 'persecutor', or the client and counsellor come to persecute each other. Counsellors who find themselves in such scenarios are well along the well-documented road towards *burnout* [27].

Testing-out
Many adults who were abused as children have painful experiences of failed relationships with others (including other counsellors) in which an almost compulsive need to test-out the other person to the point of rejection is a feature. Such *provocation of rejection* can at times, overtly or covertly, have a powerful impact on the therapeutic relationship. Testing-out is a necessary part of the process of beginning to explore and deal with concerns such as the counsellor's levels of caring, availability and his or her potential for rejection, abandonment, judgement, disbelief and loss of interest in the client. Clients may also test the counsellor's sexual boundaries.

It is through the recognition of and willingness to explore *events* in this relationship that such key themes can be identified and worked with. A simple but effective therapeutic principle is that of continually working on awareness to promote the evolution of such unconscious concerns into conscious questions. Clients grow through the experience of an increased ability and confidence to recognise and communicate such anxieties on a straightforward interpersonal level and to be able to hear clearly the response of the other.

A vital part of the therapeutic context is for the counsellor to provide and maintain safe, secure and consistent boundaries. Yet here, there is another potential counter-transference trap. The lack of consistent, appropriate and secure boundaries, as well as misuse of power and authority, is a major feature of the context of the client's original 'being abused' experience. If the counsellor responds to the client's testing-out with inconsistency, inappropriateness or is *over*-controlling *in any way*, then for the client the 'abuse-context' experience is repeated. This can occur when the counsellor's behaviour is, on one level, apparently 'helpful' and 'supportive'. However, from a counter-transference position it may be motivated by a need to be needed, need for validation, need for control, fear of the client or general discomfort with applying boundaries - saying 'no' and facing the client's frustration. Yet avoiding firmness and consistent, reasonable boundaries not only leaves the counsellor open to potentially exhausting demands, it also denies the client the opportunity of experiencing, exploring and resolving matters relating to frustration within an intimate relationship.

Many clients who were abused when they were children have experienced relationships where misuse of control has been a damaging feature. Consequently, control issues are likely to arise through transference in the therapeutic relationship. Some clients may experience the boundaries of the therapist as being uncomfortably controlling. Equally others may experience perceived weak boundaries of the therapist as being frightening. Either way, this is very important material for the therapy to address and explore.

It is important that the counsellor is able to maintain a warm but firm stance in response to testing-out, whatever form it takes. The client's task is to work out for himself or herself whether or not this person can be trusted. Reassurance or encouragement from the counsellor regarding this is unlikely to be helpful - on the basis of the maxim: *'never trust a person who says "trust me"'*. Thankfully, an effective therapeutic relationship does not require a counsellor to be perfect or superhumanly consistent. Sometimes, important exploration of transference issues occur when the counsellor has made a mistake, misunderstood, behaved inconsistently or perhaps lapsed in attentiveness. Honestly acknowledging one's fallibility and being willing to receive and accept the client's hurt or anger without becoming over-apologetic, over-compensating or rejecting in turn, can be a vital new experience for many clients.

Such interactions gradually enable people to feel confident in expressing angry or critical feelings. It may be that these have a transference source or it may be that I have been such an idiot that the response stems wholly from the client's accurate perception and appropriate response to me. Such moments provide the opportunity for learning that *the honest and open expression of difference or conflict in an intimate relationship tends to deepen that relationship in a positive way rather than to threaten it.* This can be profoundly enriching. Many adults who were abused as children are terrified of the prospect of conflict for fear that if they express differences of view or anger towards a significant other they will be perceived as bad and that rejection will follow. Through such work clients actively experiment with examining, modifying and trusting their own perceptions and learn how to communicate these clearly to another within a relationship. This provides the opportunity for rehearsal regarding the desire to develop similar accomplishments in existing or new relationships outside therapy.

Counter-transference

For the counsellor the dynamics of counter-transference are potentially equally powerful. Counter-transference also operates at a range of levels and involves the counsellor's own conscious or unconscious emotional reactions to the client based on previous life experiences. Firstly, the counsellor is likely to have emotional responses to certain *characteristics* of the client For instance, there may be a particular interest in, or distance from, certain features such as the client's type of problem, culture, age, intelligence, social class, gender or sexual orientation. There may be reactions such as irritation with the client's passivity or excessive demands; aversion to an aspect of the client's manner or attitude; flattery at expressions of gratitude and confidence in oneself; and occasions when the counsellor experiences a sexual interest or response to the client's attractiveness and implicit or explicit sexual communication.

At a second level the counsellor may have emotions, perceptions and memories which are stirred and intensified by aspects of the client's situation. This may connect with significant unfinished business in one's own personal and family history. Briere estimated that one third of female counsellors and 10-15% of male counsellors have personal histories of sexual abuse and many others will have experienced other forms of abuse and deprivation. Consequently, for all counsellors, but especially those with personal backgrounds of such trauma, it is very important that their own therapy and supervision is sufficient to maintain a constant vigilance to the question as to *what is the client's business and what is their own?* Counsellors who themselves were abused as children can, and do, make excellent and highly effective practitioners. However, when one is not clear about such divisions and boundaries there is the potential for considerable muddle and harm to be done to clients.

Typically this process involves therapists unconsciously attempting to resolve their own unfinished business *by proxy* - steering the client into, or away from, areas which connect with their own painful material. For example, a client may be led into doing work on anger or confrontation with the abuser because of the counsellor's needs; when the actual need of the client at that point may be to express sadness, loss, or the wish to maintain a distance from the abuser. With regard to such dynamics, it is worth keeping in mind another maxim, that in this relationship *the client can only travel so far as the therapist has been willing and able to go.*

It is of great concern that anecdotal reports and some research leads to the necessity to identify a psychopathological counter-transference 'type' which we might call the *abusing therapist*. Whilst it is the prerogative, right and therapeutic necessity for clients to test-out their counsellors in whatever way they need to, it is the counsellor's personal, professional and ethical responsibility not to respond in ways which are knowingly inappropriate or damaging. A number of researchers have begun to document the occurrence of sexual abuse of clients within a 'therapeutic' or other form of 'caring' relationship [28,29,30]. For example, Armsworth [31] reported that from her sample of 30 adult women who were childhood incest victims 23% of them reported that they had become sexually involved or pressured to become involved with the professionals from whom help had been sought. It is to be hoped that such exploitation of vulnerable clients, despite Armsworth's findings, is not statistically a major problem. Yet when it does occur the client is trapped in exactly the same dilemma as when a child: *'Why is this happening? Who can I tell? Will I be believed? Is it my fault? ...'*

Counter-transference responses are not simply limited to our *actions* in therapy - they also fundamentally affect what we *notice* (and do not notice) in sessions, how we perceive things, what we remember and what we forget. We are much more likely to notice, remember and respond to issues which are personally significant to ourselves. Also, the opposite is true. We are likely to miss, misperceive, ignore and forget material which is personally significant but at a less conscious level. This process can also apply at a 'world view' level: we may be emotionally open to recognising certain forms of abuse, yet less open to the existence of others. For example, despite consistent evidence from therapeutic practice, strong expressions of denial can sometimes be heard about the involvement of women as sexual abusers. For some, such abuse is a theoretical and political impossibility. Yet if such rigid opinions are held by practising counsellors, they amount to a major counter-transference *blind-spot* which can only inhibit male and female clients alike from sharing, as in this example, the experience of being sexually abused by a woman which is still largely taboo.

The appropriateness and opportunity for working directly with transference and counter-transferential material is inevitably greater in longer-term counselling. Whilst in shorter-term work the material will be manifest to some degree, the active focus is more likely to be on other aspects of the client's life experiences and relationships rather than on that with the counsellor. In work with adults who were abused as children, transference and counter-transference issues can be especially important and this often implies the need at some stage for a longer-term therapeutic relationship for their exploration and gradual resolution. Readers who feel uncertain about, or particularly interested in, this area are directed to the works of Briere[32], Cashden[33], Storr[34], Casement[35] and Hobson[36].

Shorter term counselling however can be extremely valuable, especially with regard to promoting changes in other significant relationships, the management of dissociative reactions and in telling the story.

2. Other Significant Relationships

The second major area of focus involves the client's ongoing relationships with significant others. Such relationships invariably amount to a shifting balance of supports and stresses, the occurrence and resolution of crises, the establishment of more appropriate and consistent boundaries and hopefully to a gradual increase in opportunities for sustained and rewarding intimacy.

The abusing family of origin

What is the current type and level of contact with members of the extended family? What is the effect of such contacts? Are you sure that your client is not still trapped into having sex with the abuser? This happens, and such information is not easily volunteered without a timely, tentative question from the therapist. Even if the key family members are geographically a long way away and the abuse stopped a long time ago, the controlling introjected presence of the relatives may be felt powerfully and destructively 'here and now' in a timeless and distanceless way.

If the family of origin are physically near, then it is possible that the boundaries and physical space of the client will continue to be invaded. From near or afar there may be need for action to gain some immediate control over such intrusions. This may involve practical steps such as installing an answerphone, being less responsive to correspondence and cutting out visits. We have seen how the influence of the extended family is likely to be fundamentally anti-therapeutic. Often such problems require a 'first aid' response at the very beginning of counselling. Clients can be supported in identifying short-term immediate goals, and small successes, following from planned action, can signal the beginning of the client's recognition that he or she can be effectively assertive and that further changes are possible. Such realisation provides a boost to confidence and self-esteem which generates energy for further work. However, in the process, many clients will experience a painful isolation through being ignored or 'frozen out' of the life of their extended family, whose functioning continues to be based on a collusive denial of the abuse. Lasting progress in many desired areas will only be achieved and sustained on the basis of the establishment of new relationships with the family of origin, incorporating boundaries which the client decides upon and learns to control.

Re-contacting

Work with adults abused as children inevitably involves the return to conscious awareness of repressed memories relating to abuse and the *re-association* of feelings with such memories. This can be de-stabilising. At such times, clients may have impulses towards sudden actions or initiation of contacts with significant family members. Processes relating to *re-contacting* come to the fore. The victim may feel a strong urge to visit the family to confront the abuser and others about the abuse and their part in it. It is wise to suggest caution to clients about acting on such impulses. If confrontation is to take place productively, it requires a good deal of preparation. This may involve active therapeutic work such as writing *letters not to be sent*, Gestalt work, enactment in groupwork or through visualisation. All of these techniques provide an opportunity in a safe context for the power of this material to be explored before any direct action is taken involving other family members.

This is often a phase when the experience and expression of anger is most graphically worked on. If, following on from such expressive work, the client is still of a mind to make direct contact with family members, it is important that the fantasies and expectations underlying this are examined in some detail. Victims sometimes possess a belief (which has very little evidence to support it) that if the perpetrator is confronted about the abuse, a confession and apology will follow. Similarly there may be a hope at some level of consciousness that other family members - often mothers - will acknowledge their regret at not having noticed, believed or provided protection for them in childhood.

It is crucial, if re-contacting is not to be damaging, that such hopes and expectations are examined beforehand and subjected to reality-testing. This can be done by helping the client visualise or enact possible family reactions to the visit and preparing and rehearsing their approach and response in advance for each one. Anticipation and rehearsal of responses to likely scenarios enhances the client's ability to remain in control during such emotionally intense encounters, when the ancient power of the family to pull him or her back into old roles and processes is immense.

Re-contacting, especially when ill-prepared, may lead to clients being re-abused, insulted, used as a scapegoat and banished from their families. As part of the underlying motivation often involves the infantile *yearning to be loved by one's parents,* such events are often construed as being indicators of their own personal failure and worthlessness. This can lead to significant regressions or *'nosedives'* in the progress already made. The surfacing poignancy of the primitive yearning to be loved by one's parents can be bewildering with clients in therapy unless the reality of this powerful dynamic is uncovered and acknowledged. Anniversaries such as Christmas and Mothers' Day often provoke impulsive approaches to the family. These contacts involve an abandonment of all the boundary setting work and are usually met with a punitive rejection which highlights and intensifies the despair stemming from the yearning for love and acceptance.

At such times the counsellor should gently focus on the reality: no matter how ingeniously adaptive the client may be in 'performing' for her family in the hope of gaining their acceptance nourishing and consistent love is unlikely to be forthcoming from this source. The parents are not going to change significantly at this stage of their lives: they are never going to be able to provide sufficient love. Working towards this realisation is one of the most painful stages in the therapeutic process and a vital one. It is not until the client can gradually 'let go' of the notion that denying such needs makes them go away that the process of grieving the loss of what one never had and 'settling for less' can begin. Until this occurs, the adult who was abused as a child remains in a state of timeless limbo, caught in a wholly unresolved and unrecognised grief reaction. Dealing with this loss provides the opportunity for clients to begin to experiment with allowing themselves to recognise and accept their needs and to become open to the possibility of such needs being met, if only partially, through current or future relationships.

3. Telling the Story

This is the area of work which is specific to abuse-related counselling. The healing component involves talking about the abuse to a trusted other in a safe context, whilst being able to experience, yet not be overwhelmed by, the *re-associating* emotional responses which were originally dissociated. Therapeutic work (in stages over time) may involve the return of previously repressed memories which may take the client by surprise. It may encompass re-learning how to feel: how healthily to express strong feeling and sometimes how to contain and control a flood of emotions which threaten to overwhelm. This is usually a poignant and painful time. It is vital to respect the client's own sense of the need to tell the story: when, how, how much detail and how often. Whilst there are reasons for the counsellor to proceed with caution, for some clients the pressing need may be to tell the story, and to tell it now, and to be listened to. To ignore such pressures may reinforce the client's likely early history of not being taken seriously.

In contrast, some clients are more reticent about beginning this aspect of the therapy, experiencing an inner conflict between a deep sense of needing to tell the story in the interests of healing, yet feeling acutely fearful at the prospect. For such work to be most effective it is important that it occurs when the dynamics of the therapeutic relationship are smooth and at a time when there is relative stability and available support in the client's relationships with significant others in the outside world. It is **not** a good idea to begin, or to develop, extended work on telling the story at a time of crisis. This aspect of the therapy is likely to intensify levels of emotional arousal and may promote unpredictable reactions which may stem from internal responses to original family injunctions, dissociative processes, return of unexpected memories: and a whole range of transference dynamics such as shame, guilt and mistrust of the counsellor's motives and interests.

Response to original family injunctions: We discussed earlier how the context of being abused invariably involves the introjection of powerful messages regarding secrecy and loyalty to the family. Often these are associated with threats to prevent the secret from being told. At points in therapy where the client wishes and is poised to talk about the abuse, these threats can be re-experienced internally in a very present and compelling way. The fact that this is happening may be indicated by subtle changes in facial movements, posture or mood. There may be a sudden retreat into silence, loss of eye contact, rapport; or incongruent expressions of irritation or anger with the counsellor. At such moments it can be helpful to enquire gently *'What is going on inside at the moment?'* If the phenomena of internal self-talk has already been identified, the counsellor can specifically enquire as to which voice is currently speaking and what the message is.

Such exploration often signals a revival of the original parental injunctions *not to trust* and *not to tell*. The counsellor can bring this process to the client's conscious attention, offering a graded opportunity for a small step to be taken for the client to reality-test over a period of time whether beginning to disobey such injunctions really does lead to catastrophic consequences. Hence the *pacing* of work is important. The counsellor provides a *grounding* orientation in the 'here and now' whilst the client takes the risks required to de-potentiate the old family injunctions.

Dissociative defences and remembering: In addition to material stemming from family injunctions, a major fear for many clients is of being overwhelmed by the intensity of memories and emotions. Working towards telling the story is likely to re-stimulate dissociative defences. For many clients, the experience of telling the story promotes a fear of reliving the events - flashing back into re-experience of the abuse. Post-traumatic stress responses swing between periods of re-experiencing and phases of emotional numbness. Briere describes an oscillation in the process of traumatic material being excluded from and returning to consciousness. Flashbacks and nightmares are construed as being part of a natural recovery process which occasionally and gradually allows portions of memories into conscious awareness where they can be cognitively processed and integrated, whilst at the same time allowing the client to become gradually de-sensitised to the painful feelings that are aroused. In this way flashbacks and nightmares are viewed as being representations of the mind's attempt to heal itself. This re-framing of 'symptoms' into 'healing strategies' can be a valuable positive connotation for clients who are enduring such experiences.

The challenge for the therapist is to facilitate work at the optimal emotional level - the 'affective edge' [37] - at which point the client can maintain the highest possible level of awareness of such inner processes without being triggered into dissociative defences. This may require a good deal of practice, attention to pacing and reassurance.

However, it is the client who must be in charge of how much is said, how it is said and when it is said: *"The story will be told when it is ready to be told"* [38]. Some clients who do not have a great deal of specific conscious recall of abuse find that remembering - and re-enacting - takes place spontaneously through nightmares. These often serve as a helpful barometer and 'early warning system' of repressed material bubbling upwards from the unconscious and can be positively re-framed as such. Calof uses the striking metaphorical image: *"Dreams are letters from the unconscious, nightmares are telegrams..."* [39]

Other people may be inhibited in telling the story work, not so much by difficulties in remembering the abuse but in connecting emotionally with it. Their way of protecting themselves when children was to develop the dissociative defence of emotional numbing. Effective therapeutic work is likely to employ active, expressive techniques to promote awareness and the experience of emotions. It is important to be clear that the therapeutic goal is not in itself the precipitation of mega-cathartic emotional outbursts - but the gradual integration of emotional sensation and expression into clients' lives in ways which feel congruent with their individual expectations and personalities.

The goal is the connection of emotional experience with memory and the integration of this, rather than a certain form of emotional expression for its own sake. Sometimes counsellors can subtly imply that 'heavy duty' cushion beating and pillow pounding is a necessary requirement of the healing process. For many clients it may well be. However it must *be* right and *feel* right for each client, and it must occur at the right moment. Otherwise, attempts to work in this way can compound feelings of inadequacy. If clients comply against their better inner judgement, this can constitute a further unhealthy adaptive response and can reinforce feelings of detachment and inauthenticity. Sometimes the prompting of an unprepared-for level of emotional arousal can trigger a regression back into dissociative defences. Many people make effective progress in this area, and with a greater sense of safety, by working on the expression of feelings relating to abuse material through writing, art-work, visualisation and imagery, rather than through direct physical expression.

Transference issues: Part of the therapeutic quality of telling the story is that this encompasses an experiment in and experience of trusting: voluntarily adopting a position of vulnerability (which can symbolically resemble the early 'being abused' situation) whilst taking the risk of allowing a deepening of regulated intimacy with a significant other person - the counsellor. Healing stems from the profound and repeated experience that the story does not lead to being overwhelmed, nor does it lead to being rejected, blamed, punished or exploited. Such experience gradually assuages and de-sensitises the ingrained sense of shame, through the tentatively acquired ability to remain adult-orientated and in good contact with the other, whilst communicating openly about the abuse. This may take much practice, with the counsellor giving feedback of observations such as the client's tendency to drop eye contact and to regress into childlike voices and body postures.

Clients are often in a state of heightened sensitivity regarding the counsellor at this stage of work and their perceptions will affect their internal processing of the question: *'Is this a safe person to tell my story to?'* Because of such dynamics it is always important that *telling the story* work is recognised as being significant, but that it is for each individual client to develop his or her own awareness and inner sense as to when, how and to what extent this should be undertaken. It is usually more helpful to take a neutral stance as to whether and how the story is to be told in therapy and to avoid 'pushing', unless this is with the explicit agreement of the client. If the counsellor shows persistent interest in the details of the abuse, clients may feel unease about the implications of this which could inhibit the likelihood of effective work on the abuse material.

It is unlikely, however, that most clients who were abused when they were children will reach their full recovery potential until they have in some way acquired the ability to deal directly with the abuse material in a therapeutic relationship. Healing does not arise from saying words alone but from the experience of taking the risk to do so within a new form of relationship in which the acceptance and consistency of the other counteracts the tendency towards mistrust and shame. The relationship with the counsellor will be, for many clients, the first ever experience of such quality of communication. Abuse is never forgotten. The goal is to reach the point where memories and emotional responses do not involuntarily intrude upon, overwhelm, contaminate and disable one's current experience of life and relationships: to reach the point where abuse does not constantly preoccupy present awareness and perceptions.

The ending stage of counselling will focus on the need for the client to recognise that this relationship is not *permanent* and that what has been experienced, learned and received within it must be gradually transferred onto existing and future relationships in the community. Recovery involves a gradual shift in perspective away from the familiar pain of past events into the challenge of taking - and learning to enjoy - personal responsibility for oneself. This shift from a past-orientation into a present-orientation is a gradual one and involves the subtle metamorphosis from *victim* to *survivor*.

However, many adults abused as children who have experienced the sort of therapeutic journey described in this book, discover that there is far more to life than just surviving. Healing and growth involves the discovery and expression of *creative* parts of oneself which can become deeply satisfying, alongside a developing optimistic perspective towards the future.

References

1. Anon, quoted in Sanford, L: *Strong at the Broken Places: Overcoming the trauma of childhood abuse.* Virago Press, 1991.
2. Beitchman, J, Zucker, K, Hood, J, Dacosta, G, Akman, D, & Cassavia, E: *A review of the long-term effects of child sexual abuse.* Child Abuse & Neglect. Vol.16, 101-118 (1992).
3. Clarkson, P: *Gestalt Counselling in Action.* Sage Publications, 1989.
4. Dale, P: *Dangerous families revisited.* Community Care, 14.11.91, 14-15 (1991).
5. Calof, D: *Adult survivors of incest and child abuse, part one: the family inside the adult child.* Family Therapy Today, USA, 8-16 (1988).
6. American Psychiatric Association: *Diagnostic & Statistical Manual of Mental Disorders (DSM-111-R).* APA, 1987.
7. Briere, J: *Therapy for Adults Molested as Children: Beyond Survival.* Springer Publishing Co., New York, 1989.
8. Speigel, H: *The dissociation-association continuum.* Paper at 8th International Conference on Multiple Personality/Dissociative States. Chicago, 1991.
9. Speigel, H: *The dissociation-association continuum.* Paper at 8th International Conference on Multiple Personality/Dissociative States. Chicago, 1991.
10. Briere, J: *Therapy for Adults Molested as Children: Beyond Survival.* Springer Publishing Co., New York, 1989.
11. Educational Media International: *To a Safer Place.* National Film Board, Canada, 1987.
12. Stewart, I: *Transaction Analysis Counselling in Action.* Sage Publications, 1989.
13. Rowan, J: *Subpersonalities: The People Inside Us.* Routledge, 1990.
14. Ferrucci, P: *What We May Be: The Visions & Techniques of Psychosynthesis.* Turnstone Press, 1982.
15. Karpman, S: *Fairy tales and script drama analysis.* Transactional Analysis Bulletin Vol. 7, No. 26, 39-43, 1968.
16. Gil, E: *Outgrowing the Pain.* Launch Press, San Francisco, 1983.
17. Maltz, W & Holman, B: *Incest & Sexuality: A Guide to Understanding & Healing.* Lexington Books, 1987.
18. Bolton, F, Morris, L & MacEachron, A: *Males at Risk: The Other Side of Sexual Abuse.* Sage Publications, 1989.
19. Dale, P & Locke, V: *Group counselling for adults abused as children: reflections on theory and group process.* (In preparation).
20. Frenken, J & Van Stolk, B: *Incest victims: inadequate help by professionals.* Child Abuse & Neglect, Vol. 14, No. 2, 253-263, 1990.

21. Armsworth, M: *Therapy of incest survivors: abuse or support?* Child Abuse & Neglect, Vol. 13, No. 4, 549-562, 1989.
22. Langs, R: *A Primer of Psychotherapy.* New York: Jason Aronsen, 1988.
23. Cashden, S: *Object Relations Therapy: Using the Relationship.* W.W. Norton, 1988.
24. Casement, P: *On Learning from the Patient.* Routledge, 1986.
25. Storr, A: *The Art of Psychotherapy.* Butterworth Heinmann, 2nd edition, 1990.
26. Briere, J: *Therapy for Adults Molested as Children: Beyond Survival.* Springer Publishing Co., New York, 1989.
27. Dale, P, Davies, M, Morrison, T & Waters, J: *Dangerous Families.* Tavistock Publications, London, 1986. See Chapter 9: Professional Survival.
28. Rutter, P: *Sex in the Forbidden Zone.* Mandala Books, London, 1991.
29. Armsworth, M: *A qualitative analysis of adult incest survivors' responses to sexual involvement with therapists.* Child Abuse & Neglect, Vol. 14, No. 4, 541-554, 1990.
30. Masson, J: *Against Therapy.* Fontana, 1990.
31. Armsworth, M: *Therapy of incest survivors: abuse or support?* Child Abuse & Neglect, Vol. 13, No. 4, 549-562, 1989.
32. Briere, J: *Therapy for Adults Molested as Children: Beyond Survival.* Springer Publishing Co., New York, 1989.
33. Cashdan, S: *Object Relations Therapy: Using the Relationship.* W.W. Norton, 1988.
34. Storr, A: *The Art of Psychotherapy.* Butterworth Heinmann, 2nd edition, 1990.
35. Casement, P: *On Learning from the Patient.* Routledge, 1986.
36. Hobson, R: *Forms of Feeling: The Heart of Psychotherapy.* Tavistock Publications, London, 1986.
37. Cornell, WF & Olio, KA: *Integrating effect in treatment with adult survivors of physical and sexual abuse.* American Journal of Orthopsychiatry, Vol. 61(1), 59-69, 1991.
38. Calof, D: *UK Training Workshop.* 1988
39. Calof, D: *UK Training Workshop.* 1988
40. Woods, SC & Dean, KS: *Final Report: Sexual abuse of males research project.* Quoted in Bolton, Morris & MacEachron.

Further Reading

Helpful Books for Clients:

Gil, E: *Outgrowing the Pain: A book for and about adults abused as children.* Launch Press, Walnut Creek, California, 1983.

Forward, S: *Toxic Parents: Overcoming the legacy of parental abuse.* Bantam Press, London, 1990.

Parks, P: *Rescuing the 'Inner Child': Therapy for adults sexually abused as children.* Souvenir Press, London, 1990.

Thomas, T: *Victims No Longer: Men recovering from incest and other sexual child abuse.* Launch Press, Walnut Creek, California, 1989.

Key books on causation and consequences of abuse:

Butler, S: *Conspiracy of Silence: The trauma of incest.* New Glide Publications, San Francisco, 1978.

Meiselman, KC: *Incest: A Psychological Study of causes and effects with treatment recommendations.* Jossey-Bass Publishers, San Francisco, 1978.

Herman, JL: *Father-Daughter Incest.* Harvard University Press, 1981.

Finklehor, D: *Child Sexual Abuse: New Theory & Research.* The Free Press, New York, 1984.

Miller, A: *For Your Own Good: The Roots of Violence in Child Rearing.* Virago Press, London, 1984.

Bass, E & Davis, L: *The Courage to Heal.* Harper & Row, New York, 1988.

Hall, I & Lloyd, S: *Surviving Child Sexual Abuse.* Falmer Press, London, 1989.

Sanford, L: *Strong at the Broken Places: Overcoming the Trauma of Childhood Abuse.* Virago Press, London, 1991.

Males:

Bolton, FG Jr, Morris, LA & MacEachron, AE: *Males at Risk: The other side of child sexual abuse.* Sage Publications, 1989.

Lew, M: *Victims no Longer: Men recovering from incest and other sexual child abuse.* Harper & Row, New York, 1988.

Key books on abuse-related therapy/counselling:

Briere, J: *Therapy for Adults Molested as Children: Beyond Survival.* Springer Publishing Co., New York, 1989.

Gil, E: *Treatment of Adult Survivors of Childhood Abuse.* Launch Press, Walnut Creek, California, 1988.

Courtois, C: *Healing the Incest Wound: Adult Survivors in Therapy.* W.W. Norton, New York, 1988.

Sanderson, C: *Counselling Adult Survivors of Child Sexual Abuse.* Jessica Kingsley, London, 1990.

Jehu, D: *Beyond Sexual Abuse: Therapy with Women who were Childhood Victims.* John Wiley, Chichester, 1988.

Maltz, W & Holman, B: *Incest & Sexuality: A Guide to Understanding & Healing.* Lexington Books, Lexington USA, 1987.

Autobiographical Accounts:

Spring, J: *Cry Hard & Swim: The Story of an Incest Survivor.* Virago Press, London, 1987.

Schreiber, FR: *Sybil.* Henry Regnery Co., Chicago, 1973.

Chase, T: *When Rabbit Howls.* Pan Books, London, 1988.

Fraser, S: *My Father's House: A Memoir of Incest & Healing.* Virago Press, London, 1989.

Educational Media International: *To a Safer Place.* National Film Board, Canada, 1987.